Countries of the World

Brazil

by Michael Dahl

Bridgestone Books

an Imprint of Capstone Press

Bridgestone Books are published by Capstone Press
151 Good Counsel Drive, P.O. Box 669, Mankato, Minnesota 56002
http://www.capstone-press.com

Library of Congress Cataloging-in-Publication Data
Dahl, Michael
    Brazil/by Michael Dahl.
    p.   cm.—(Countries of the world)
    Includes bibliographical references and index.
    Summary: An introduction to the geography, history, people, and culture of Brazil, the largest country in
South America.
    ISBN 1-56065-522-4
    1. Brazil—Juvenile literature. [1. Brazil] I. Title. II. Series: Countries of the world (Mankato, Minn.)
    F2508.5.D34   1997
    981—dc21   96-50161
                                                                                                      CIP
                                                                                                      AC

Bridgestone Books would like to thank the education department of the Embassy of Brazil in
Washington, D.C., for their help with this project.

Photo Credits
Michelle Coughlan, 5 (right)
Betty Crowell, 10
Flag Research Center, 5 (left)
FPG, 18; Haroldo Castro, 20
International Stock/George Ancona, cover; Al Clayton, 8
Unicorn/Jeff Greenberg, 14; Doris Brookes, 16
Visuals Unlimited/Max and Bea Hunn, 6; Andreozzi, 12

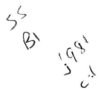

Table of Contents

Fast Facts

Name: Brazil
Capital: Brasília
Population: More than 158 million
Language: Portuguese
Religion: Roman Catholic, Protestant, Candomblé

Size: 3,286,470 square miles (8,544,822 square kilometers)
Brazil is a little larger than the lower 48 states of the United States.

Crops: Coffee, cotton

Maps

Brazil

VENEZUELA GUYANA
SURINAME
FRENCH GUIANA
COLOMBIA
North Atlantic Ocean
The Amazon River
PERU
BOLIVIA
Brasília ★
PARAGUAY
Rio de Janeiro
São Paulo
South Atlantic Ocean
CHILE
South Pacific Ocean
ARGENTINA
URUGUAY

▲ Andes Mountain Range

Brazil

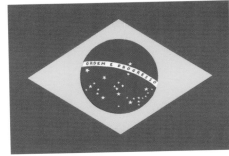

Flag

The background color of Brazil's flag is green. Green stands for Brazil's forests. There is a yellow diamond in the flag's center. This stands for the many minerals found there. In the middle of the diamond, there is a blue globe. Inside the globe, there are 27 stars. The stars are arranged like the night sky over Brazil. There is a star for each state and one for the federal district of Brazil. The white band across the globe stands for order and progress.

Currency

Brazil's unit of currency is the real. Each real is broken into centavos. A centavo is similar to a U.S. penny. It takes 100 centavos to equal a real.

One Brazilian real is almost equal to one U.S. dollar.

Rain Forest, Farm, and City

Brazil is the largest country in South America. It is also the fifth-largest country in the world. It is larger than the lower 48 states of the United States. Brazil has 26 states.

The river Amazon flows through northern Brazil. It is the second-longest river in the world. The world's largest tropical rain forest surrounds the Amazon. For half of the year, it rains every day in the forest.

Southern Brazil is covered by wetlands, farms, and mountains. Brazil's farms grow most of the world's coffee. Mountains lie along Brazil's ocean coast. Giant cities are squeezed between Brazil's mountains and the ocean shore.

Brazil's ocean coast is covered with mountains.

The Amazon

The river Amazon begins in the Andes Mountains of Peru. Peru is one of Brazil's neighbors.

The Amazon flows east for 4,000 miles (6,400 kilometers). Hundreds of small rivers flow into the Amazon. Then the Amazon empties into the Atlantic Ocean.

A wall of water rises where the Amazon meets the Atlantic. The wall of water is called a bore. Sometimes it is as high as 15 feet (four and one-half meters).

Once it was hard for people to travel through the Amazon rain forest. So Brazil built a long road to help travelers. The road is called the Trans-Amazon highway. It crosses through the huge rain forest.

A huge rain forest surrounds the Amazon.

Going to School

Brazil has both public and private schools. Children go to school from age seven through age 14. Public school is free for students.

Students wear uniforms at school. Usually, it is a T-shirt with the school's name on it.

Children go to school in four-hour blocks. Their block can be in the morning or the afternoon. There are night classes for adults, too.

Progress in school depends on classroom hours attended. It does not depend on school years. That way, working students can learn at their own rate.

Students who want to attend college must pass the vestibular (vehs-tee-boo-LAHR). It is a test that is given every year. Students study very hard to pass the test.

Students wear T-shirts with the school's name on them.

Brazilian Homes

About three-fourths of all Brazilians live in cities. Houses in Brazilian cities are similar to North American homes.

Many Brazilians move to cities to find work. So apartment buildings add more floors to their tops. This makes them very tall. But it helps people find places to live.

In the country, farmers and ranchers live in wooden houses. Village people have houses made of stone or dried mud. The roofs are made of bright-orange tiles.

Near the Amazon, Indians make homes from reeds and cane. Reeds and cane are plants found in the area. The Indians sleep in hammocks above the ground.

Some Indians make homes from reeds and cane.

Brazilian Food

Many different kinds of people live in Brazil. Brazilian food is a mix of their many ways of cooking.

The most important meal for Brazilians is lunch. For lunch, they usually eat meat stew. It is served with rice and beans. Rice and black beans are part of every meal.

Most Brazilians eat feijoada (fay-jhoo-AH-dah) every Saturday. This meal combines dried and smoked meats with black beans.

Farofa (fah-ROH-fah) is served with the feijoada. Farofa is made of fried manioc flour. Manioc is a common Brazilian food. It comes from a tropical plant. Its roots are pounded into flour for bread.

Seafood is also popular in Brazil. Shrimp is a popular snack. People catch many kinds of fish in Brazil's rivers.

Shrimp is a popular snack in Brazil.

Brazilian Animals

More than 1,600 kinds of birds live in Brazil. This is more than any country in the world. Toucans and colorful parrots live in the trees.

Monkeys swing from tree branches in the rain forest. Anteaters nose the ground for ants. Many kinds of turtles, lizards, snakes, and alligators also live there.

There are 1,500 kinds of fish in Brazil's rivers. The pirarucu (pur-AR-oo-koo) is one of the largest fishes in the world. It grows up to six and one-half feet (two meters) long. It weighs about 275 pounds (125 kilograms).

Piranha fish live in the river, too. Their teeth are razor sharp. Piranha can chew off a person's leg in seconds. Luckily, they usually do not attack humans.

The teeth of a piranha fish are razor sharp.

Soccer and Carnival

The favorite sport in Brazil is soccer. They call it futebol (FUT-bal). People play it all year long. The city of Rio de Janeiro has the world's largest sports stadium. Maracanã Stadium can hold 200,000 futebol fans.

Edson Arantes do Nascimento is one of the world's greatest futebol players. He is also known as Pele. Pele was born in Brazil. He helped Brazil win the World Cup futebol championship three times.

Every year, Brazilians have a celebration called Carnival. Many people do not work for four days. There is a big parade with beautiful floats.

During Carnival, people wear fancy costumes and dance all night long. They dance to the heavy beat of samba (SAHM-bah). Samba is a type of Brazilian music.

People wear fancy costumes during Carnival.

Brasília and São Paulo

Brasília is Brazil's capital. It was built in the middle of wilderness. Its buildings have a modern design. It opened in 1960.

São Paulo is Brazil's largest city. Seven million people live there. This makes it the seventh-largest city in the world. São Paulo is home to many kinds of businesses. People go there to find work.

Brazil has cut down on pollution in its cities. Many of Brazil's cars do not use gasoline for fuel. Instead, they use alcohol made from sugar cane for fuel.

Underground trains are the easiest way to travel through cities. These trains are called subways. Subways travel through large tubes underneath the crowded streets.

São Paulo is Brazil's largest city.

Hands On: Play Peteca

Some people in Brazil like to play this game at parties.

What you need:

small beanbag or sock
sand
three feathers
string

Playing the Game:

1. Fill your beanbag or sock with sand.
2. Get your string. Use it to tie the feathers. Tie the feathers to the top of the beanbag or sock.
3. Toss the bag into the air.
4. Say a letter of the alphabet or a number. You do this every time you hit the bag into the air.
5. Wait for the bag to come down. Use your hand to hit it back into the air. Hit it before it touches the ground. Do this as many times as you can.
6. You lose your turn if the bag touches the ground. You also lose your turn if you forget to say a letter or a number.
7. You win the game by saying the most letters or numbers. You say these before the ball touches the ground.

Learn to Speak Portuguese

good-bye	tchau	(CHOW)
hello	oi	(OY)
help	socorro	(soh-KORE-oh)
no	não	(NOU)
please	por favor	(PORE fah-VORE)
that's great	chocante	(choh-KAHN-tee)
yes	sim	(SEEM)

Words to Know

Amazon (AM-uh-zahn)—the second-longest river in the world; flows through South America

bore (BOR)—a wall of water made when two bodies of water flow into each other

manioc (ma-NEE-ahk)—a tropical plant whose roots are ground into flour to make bread and other foods

piranha (pur-AH-nah)—a meat-eating fish

pirarucu (pur-AR-oo-koo)—one of the largest fish in the world

rain forest (RAYN FOR-ist)—forest of tall trees that grows where it is warm and rainy all year

samba (sahm-BAH)—Brazilian music with a heavy beat

Read More

Enderlein, Cheryl L. *Celebrating Birthdays in Brazil.* Birthdays around the World. Mankato, Minn.: Hilltop Books, 1998.

Forsyth, Adrian. *How Monkeys Make Choclate: Foods and Medicines from the Rain Forest.* Toronto: Grey de Pencier Books Inc., 1995.

O'Mara, Anna. *Rain Forests.* Mankato, Minn.: Bridgestone Books, 1996.

Weitzman, Elizabeth. *Brazil.* Minneapolis: Carolrhoda Books, 1998.

Useful Addresses and Internet Sites

Embassy of Brazil
3006 Massachusetts Avenue NW
Washington, DC 20008

Pen Pal Planet
P.O. Box 20111
Scranton, PA 18502

Brazilian Embassy in Washington
http://www.brasil.emb.nw.dc.us

Brazil InfoNet
http://www.brazilinfo.net

Index